The Yellow Book 2015

by Peter Hirst & Claire Ramsbotham of 'rethinkyourmind'

Develop-Insite CIC
57 Cambridge Road, Sawbridgeworth
Hertfordshire CM21 9JP

Published in the United Kingdom by:

Develop-Insite CIC
57 Cambridge Road, Sawbridgeworth
Hertfordshire CM21 9JP

www.rethinkyourmind.co.uk

Full copyright © Develop-Insite CIC. All rights reserved.

A CIP record of this book is available from the British Library.

The Yellow Book 2015 was first printed in June 2015.
ISBN 978-0-9932972-0-5

rethinkyourmind.co.uk

Contents

8   Wellbeing section - The Centre of Wellbeing

36   Recovery section - The Institute of Psychiatry, Psychology & Neuroscience

38   Recovery section - ImROC

40   Recovery section - The Royal College of Psychiatrists

42   Recovery section - NHS Choices

45   Panel of Assessors for Poetry and Art

57   Poetry and Artwork Selected Entries

111 National Supporters

138 Thanks

Should you require urgent help, please call:
The Samaritans: 08457 90 90 90 ChildLine: 0800 11 11 (24 hours)

rethinkyourmind.co.uk

Welcome

Dear Reader

This book has been put together with the intention that it will enhance the lives of those that choose to read it. You are holding this book in your hands thanks to all the wonderful and selfless people that have supported this venture.

I have been through very challenging times with my mental health, which in turn affected my family and friends. I was admitted to hospital several times in my early 20's spending nearly 11 months in total on the wards before being diagnosed with bipolar.

During a strong journey of recovery with the support of SISO and Advance, I was inspired to create a resource that brings a sense of connectedness into a subject that can often be very disconnecting.

After many years of support I am now delighted to have moved on to become the joint owner of the 'not for profit' company: Develop-Insite CIC alongside Claire Ramsbotham who owns The Centre of Wellbeing. Our vision is to facilitate the continued growth of rethinkyourmind and The Yellow Book and to ensure their sustainability.

Being creative with music through singing and writing with 'refuge' has been a key factor to maintaining my wellbeing and contributed hugely to why the project supports positive mental health through creativity.

The Wellbeing material developed by The Centre of Wellbeing for this publication is wonderful. Everyone's journey is unique and I feel that the more options that are available in challenging times the better. I live in deepest gratitude to all my family, friends and colleagues who have supported me in my role and on my journey.

In Kindness
Pete Hirst
Rethinkyourmind: Project Manager & Creator
Develop-Insite CIC: Joint Owner

Foreword

Wellbeing matters. We know that poor mental wellbeing can have an impact on every area of our daily lives – it can have a negative impact on our physical health, it can affect our work, our relationships and our families – and it can sometimes last a lifetime.

Yet good mental wellbeing can help us achieve our goals in life and is associated with positive outcomes such as social connectedness, educational achievement, and maintaining a home, a job and relationships.

So, what is good mental wellbeing and how do we achieve it? There are many factors that can influence our wellbeing.

In Britain, we have become richer and we have more money to spend on possessions and holidays, but evidence has shown that this does not necessarily lead to increased happiness or improved wellbeing.

Foreword

Evidence has shown that the actions we take and the way we think will have the biggest impact - this is the way to improve how we feel about ourselves and our lives. In other words, we can achieve wellbeing through creativity and active community participation to give us a purpose and to generate an overall positive outlook on life.

The winning artists and artworks in this book powerfully demonstrate this and make it unequivocal - the more we put into our lives, the more we are likely to get out.

Professor Lord Patel of Bradford
OBE

Foreword

Opening the simple yellow cover, I can flick to any page of this book and find inspirational images; uplifting words and a world of support. It is a compact resource that fully embraces the diversity and individuality of each of its readers.

I, personally, believe it is important that we focus on what we can do and that we build on our strengths so it was good to hear that this year's 'rethinkyourmind' entries were created around the statement:

'I feel better when I am...'

280 entries, from all over the country, were received in total and a selection of 50 motivating pieces of art, photography and poetry now reside here for readers to browse and trial.

'The Yellow Book' ticks so many boxes and I am confident that you will discover its many benefits during the time you spend immersed in its pages.

We are delighted to be supporting 'rethinkyourmind' and The Yellow Book.

Dr Geraldine Strathdee,
NHS England's National Clinical Director for Mental Health

Foreword

People who use mental health services have told us the best treatment is being able to maintain control over their lives and symptoms and having the opportunity to build a life beyond their illness. Recovery is about maintaining control, but also about finding and keeping a job, having somewhere safe to live, developing supportive relationships with family and friends and working in partnership with health and social care providers.

Recovery-focused practice celebrates an individual's strengths and achievements, whilst providing access to support mechanisms that suit their needs. Adopting a recovery approach in service delivery is something providers will need to tackle sooner or later if we really are going to improve quality and improve outcomes for the people who use our services.

Rethink Your Mind demonstrates the importance of celebrating an individual's strength at times of adversity and offers valuable information to help people rebuild and enhance the quality of their lives.

Stephen Dalton
Chief Executive Mental Health Network

Foreword

Welcome to this fantastic collection of poetry, artwork and photography, all inspired by the words:

"I Feel Better When I Am..."

We are all familiar with the positive benefits that arts projects can bring to people's mental health, and the Royal College of Psychiatrists has long been a supporter of mental health and the arts.

Fourteen years ago The Royal College of Psychiatrists' arts initiative '2001: A Mind Odyssey' helped raise awareness of the therapeutic benefits of artistic expression, and since then has been involved in a number of mental health-themed plays, exhibitions and events.

The book you are holding is a unique celebration of creativity and the mind, and bursts with messages of positivity, recovery and wellbeing.

I have been hugely inspired by the winning submissions, and I hope other psychiatrists and mental health professionals will feel the same.

Professor Dame Sue Bailey OBE DBE
Immediate Past President of the Royal College of Psychiatrists, Chair, Academy of Medical Royal Colleges

Foreword

The international understanding of recovery is changing. It used to be thought that recovery means getting rid of un-valued experiences, such as symptoms. This understanding has been challenged by people with lived experience (such as hearing voices and having emotional difficulties), who assert their right to be citizens without needing to first become 'normal'.

This new approach – personal recovery – involves finding a life beyond illness. Personal recovery involves adding, not taking away: creating new layers of positive identity; amplifying the use of personal strengths and social resources; learning that one has something to offer as well as needing support from others; and discovering that lived experience can be an asset, not a vulnerability.

The art and poetry in this book illustrate the transformation from mental illness to interesting, idiosyncratic, creative, flawed, learning, contributing, changing personhood.

This book illuminates some key processes in the journey to personal recovery and wellbeing.

Professor Mike Slade
Institute of Psychiatry, Psychology & Neuroscience, King's College London

Introduction

Hello and welcome to the Wellbeing section of the Yellow Book!

All of the content here was created after discussion with a wonderful group of friends that include service users, carers, and wellbeing professionals. Each person involved truly values the Yellow Book as a perfect way of sharing experience and 'giving back'.

It is our hope that these wellbeing tools will give you the opportunity to explore some different ideas for managing stress or simply remind you of practices that you may have forgotten in the noise of daily living.

Often, we refer to these tools as practices because it can take time to get used to them and because they usually become easier, the more regularly we feel able to practise them.

These pages are yours to simply flick through and see what catches your eye, allowing yourself this time to relax and to focus on your wellbeing.

These practices are our gift to you, to make your own and inspire you along your wellbeing journey, with our very best wishes.

www.thecentreofwellbeing.co.uk

Wellbeing

THE CENTRE OF WELLBEING

The Power of Awareness

Imagine that you are walking down the street and you see a friend on the other side and you wave but they don't acknowledge you... take a minute to consider how this makes you feel.

- It is likely that on a sunny day that has unravelled smoothly, you'd laugh it off and believe your friend hadn't seen you!

- Whilst on a morning of feeling tired, stressed & developing cold symptoms, you might feel more upset by the experience and believe that you have done something to upset your friend.

> It always seems impossible until it's done
>
> ~ Nelson Mandela

 THE CENTRE OF WELLBEING

Wellbeing

Neither reaction is right or wrong but they illustrate that an experience changes depending on our reaction which can vary from person to person, day to day and moment to moment.

Our reactions often happen automatically so stop and allow a brief pause before choosing how to respond and, in most cases, manage the stress response more beneficially.

Remember that responding instead of reacting takes practise and be patient with yourself.

Wellbeing

Quietening the mind

We know that the mind sometimes has a habit of being very distracting but truly, it's OK if your mind wanders when doing these practices, when you notice it's happened, finish the thought and then actively return your focus to the practice. (Let go of getting cross with yourself, as this will simply become a distraction).

- **Practice:** Use your breath as an anchor which means that you simply observe it. Nothing at all for you to do other than watch the breath and the body as it breathes…

- **Practice:** Sit with a burning candle and watch the flame dance. It's a very absorbing practice and requires only a few minutes.

- **Practice:** Focus on your big toe so that nothing else exists! Immerse yourself in awareness of that big toe, noticing how it feels & any sensations and then release it into peaceful relaxation. Continue with the rest of the toes if you wish…

THE CENTRE OF WELLBEING

Wellbeing

Feedback from our friends

"I honestly believed my thoughts would never be quiet but by allowing my thoughts & letting go of my resistance, things are changing! My best advice to you is keep practising!"

~Lisa Bayford

"Once I allowed myself the time to be still and quiet, my thoughts began to quieten too. Now, I feel calmer and my mind is definitely clearer and I can choose what I think about."

~Jacob Davine

Wellbeing

THE CENTRE OF WELLBEING

Your words are your wand!

The words you think; the words you write down and the words you say all affect the way you feel and how you experience life.

- **Practice:**

Notice how it feels when you say:

I am smiling

Now let that feeling pass and say:

I am frowning

Perhaps, you felt your body respond to these words and you began to physically smile or frown.

Perhaps you noticed a shift in your feelings depending on whether you were saying that you were smiling or frowning.

There's no right or wrong answer to this, it is simply a way to illustrate the power of our words.

Be careful how you are talking to yourself because you are listening.

~Lisa M Hayes

Feedback from our friends

"Three little words that made my life feel unbearable at times, were: guilt, blame and regret. Over time, I chose instead to let go of these words and remember that: 1. I'm human. 2. I'm learning and 3. I'm doing my best. I truly believe that our life experience can be altered by our choice of words!"

~Natalie Vernon

THE CENTRE OF WELLBEING   Wellbeing

Helpful ideas:

- First thing in the morning or last thing at night, take a pen and empty all that you wish onto the blank pages of a journal – simply let it flow freely, you may never read what you've written but the idea is that you'll feel better for letting it all out!

- Before you say something out loud, run it in your head – make a conscious choice about what you say to others.

- Write some words on post-it notes that encourage your practice and leave them around your home to help keep you feeling energised. e.g. Awareness, Patience, Respond

- If you like to read, choose books that build your vocabulary with interesting and empowering words.

- Sing! In the shower, in the car, wherever works for you! Music is a wonderful tool for switching our moods and raising our energy.

Be Gentle with Yourself

Often we can be more gentle and understanding with others than we are with ourselves.

Kindness towards ourselves can be a helpful way to redress the balance.

- **Practice:**

Simply sit in a comfortable and relaxed position. Take two or three deep breaths.

Now silently repeat:

"May I be happy - May I be well - May I be safe - May I be peaceful and at ease".

As you say each phrase, allow yourself to notice how you feel.

Repeat as you wish.

After a period of directing loving-kindness toward yourself, you may wish to expand the practice to others but only if you feel ready to do so.

When you are practising kindness towards people you care about, firstly, bring them to mind and then silently repeat:

"May you be happy - May you be well - May you be safe - May you be peaceful & at ease".

Repeat as you wish.

Alternatively, you can practise kindness towards animals, forests, deserts, beaches or any other element of nature with which you feel connected.

> "Kindness is the language that the deaf can hear and the blind can see."
>
> ~ *Mark Twain*

THE CENTRE OF WELLBEING   Wellbeing

Feedback from our friends

"I find practising 'loving-kindness' really helps me to be kinder to myself, it has genuinely quietened that inner voice that has often been my harshest critic"

~Sarah Jane Franklin

"The idea of sending loving kindness seemed rather unnatural initially but when I realised that the intention of 'Metta' practice was to open my own heart, it became immediately real"

~Gary Baxter

"This practice surprised me, it really soothed my feelings of resistance and supported me in letting go of some emotional baggage – have a go, you'll be pleased you did!"

~Beverley Challis

Share your feedback at:

www.rethinkyourmind.co.uk/feedback

Next time, we may be able to include your comments in The Yellow Book.

THE CENTRE OF WELLBEING   Wellbeing

> "Life can be found only in the present moment."
>
> ~ Thich Nhat Hanh

The HERE and NOW

You've probably heard the phrase: 'Life is a journey not a destination' this is what is meant by living in the present moment.

It's about choosing to enjoy every moment that leads to the destination so that the mundane parts of life become far more interesting and you naturally feel more content.

Living in the moment is often referred to as mindfulness and these practices illustrate ways we can live more mindfully:-

- **Practice:** take a shower and enjoy each and every drop of water as it touches your skin, inhale the scent of your toiletries, allow yourself to experience every moment as if it was the first shower you'd ever taken.

The alternative is that we often shower with lots of other people!! Yes it's true! We often play out our day and focus all our energies on running through conversations with people that we most likely would not like to join us in the shower! Food for thought perhaps?...

- **Practice:** make up your own mindful practice around an everyday routine of your choice e.g cleaning your teeth, drinking a cup of tea, walking down the stairs etc…

Remember it's all about the experience…

Wellbeing　　　　　　　　　　THE CENTRE OF WELLBEING

Affirmations

These are short phrases that you can write down or say to yourself.

They have a positive focus and are written in the present and are useful tools to begin shifting our perceptions, habits and mindsets.

How to create your own affirmations:
Consider how you would like to feel today…
Now write down a short statement that reflects this:
e.g. 'I am enjoying every moment of this day, in every way'.

Let this statement be your daily affirmation!
Start your day with it & bring it to mind throughout the day.
Then, when you reflect on your day at bedtime change it to:
e.g. 'I enjoyed every moment of this day, in every way'.

Notice how your affirmation begins to shift your behaviour…

Be patient though!

Remember that we have to repeat something at least 21 times, before we begin to break the habit!

We recommend seeking additional support if you find that after 30 days, you have experienced no change.

THE CENTRE OF WELLBEING					Wellbeing

Feedback from our friends

"I found affirmations a little hard to do at first because they felt contrived so I decided to simply be thankful. By affirming my gratitude throughout my day, I found more and more things to be grateful about! It's a really rewarding practice."

~Michelle Tohill

Wellbeing

THE CENTRE OF WELLBEING

Feeling Safe

This meditation is simple and can be used whenever it feels helpful to be in our own, imagined 'safe space' and we can visit it whenever we wish.

"Life is a balance of holding on and letting go."

~Lisa M Hayes

- Practice:

1. Take 3 deep breaths and allow your full attention to fall upon the rising and falling of your chest.

2. Remember that the body and breath are always in the present moment and so concentrating on them stops the cycle of past behaviour or future worry.

3. Whether you're sitting or lying down, let your body become heavy and surrender to relaxation.

THE CENTRE OF WELLBEING

Wellbeing

4. As you let go of the noise and allow yourself to relax deeper, bring to mind a place that you feel is your 'safe space'. This place can be somewhere you've visited, seen in a picture or literally imagined on the spot.

5. Take time to create all the detail of this place in your imagination, include smells, tastes, colours, sounds, textures etc

6. When you feel content that you have created a 'safe space' which is all your own, create a comfy area where you can lie or sit down and just rest and breathe in the peace.

7. Stay in this space for as long as you wish and when you feel it's time, slowly bring your attention back to the room in which you sit or lie by opening your eyes.

THE CENTRE OF WELLBEING

Wellbeing

Gratitude

"The miracle of gratitude is that it shifts your perception to such an extent that it changes the world that you see."

~ Dr Robert Holden

How about making yourself a gratitude jar?...

Each day that you feel able, write down at least one thing that you are thankful for on a piece of coloured paper and pop it in the jar.

When you're not feeling so thankful, you can dip into the jar and remember all the things that you appreciate.

Feedback from our friends

"When I focus on expressing gratitude, my awareness of my surroundings is heightened. Appreciation for all that we have is a powerful way to attract more of the same."

~Pete Hirst

Wellbeing   THE CENTRE OF WELLBEING

Stretch!

Stretching is the body's way of reducing tension that has built up in your muscles and you can use it whenever & wherever you choose:

- Feel, in your body, where the tension is coming from.
- Allow your body to move and stretch out from that tightness until it settles.
- The time it takes and the movements that come will be different each time you stretch, as your body's needs are always changing.
- Give yourself time to finish a stretch, to maximise the benefit.
- If you find that you are holding your breath during a stretch; just slowly breathe out as the stretch relaxes.
- Stretching into pain will make your muscles tighten up again so is not advisable. Remember to seek medical advice if you have undiagnosed pain

This daily practice will become natural eventually but in the early stages, be patient with the process and learn to trust your body; it knows what it's doing!

Tap your way to Wellbeing!

This Practice works on the basis that disruptions to the body's energy system result in negative emotions. It is often referred to as EFT which stands for Emotional Freedom Technique.

This technique involves tapping on certain meridian points in the body whilst feeling & acknowledging emotions in order to allow us to let go of the emotion

We have focused on the Faster EFT technique here to act as a simple introduction to tapping.

Feedback from our friends

"I use EFT whenever I feel my anxiety levels rising, I feel overwhelmed by life or other people. It is a quick, easy and effective self-help tool to both relieve the negativity but also to instil more positivity!"

~Carol May

"After many years of physical and emotional pain from rheumatoid arthritis and lupus I came across tapping & found it really easy to do. The benefits were almost instant! Slowly I felt better as I practised every day... Eventually, I followed my passion of this simple technique and became an EFT practitioner & now support others by passing on this practice."

~Linda Swanton

Wellbeing

THE CENTRE OF WELLBEING

5 Basic Steps to Tapping:
1. Identify the Emotion

Choose an emotion from the 'emotional scale' below:

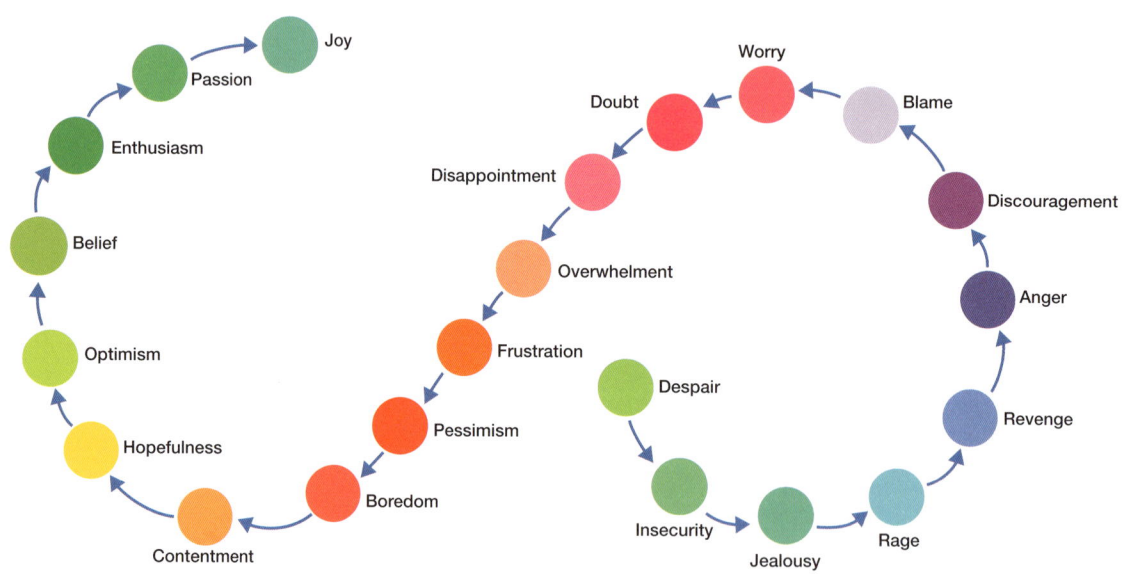

2. Test the Intensity:

Before you begin tapping, consider the intensity of this feeling on a scale of 1-10 where 10 is the strongest – this is your 'before' level.

3. The Setup:

This is a simple phrase which you say while continuously tapping the 'karate chop' point (See inset picture below).

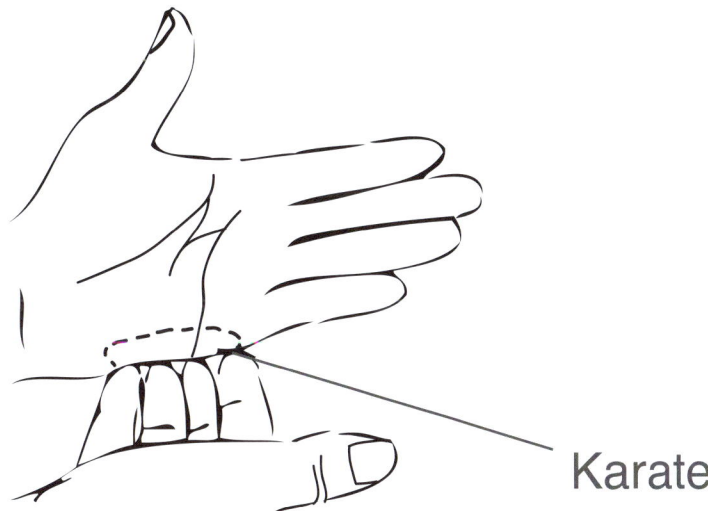

When designing this phrase:

1) Acknowledge the emotion &

2) Accept yourself in spite of it, by saying:

"Even though I have this feeling of ……… I deeply and completely accept myself and how I feel".
Note: Be clear about the negative emotion. This allows our natural positives to bubble up to the top.

Wellbeing   THE CENTRE OF WELLBEING

4. The Sequence:

This is the workhorse part that stimulates/balances the body's energy pathways. To perform it, you tap each of the points shown in the diagram (see below) while saying a reminder phrase that keeps your body tuned into the emotion.

"Even though I have this feeling of …………… I deeply and completely accept myself and how I feel".

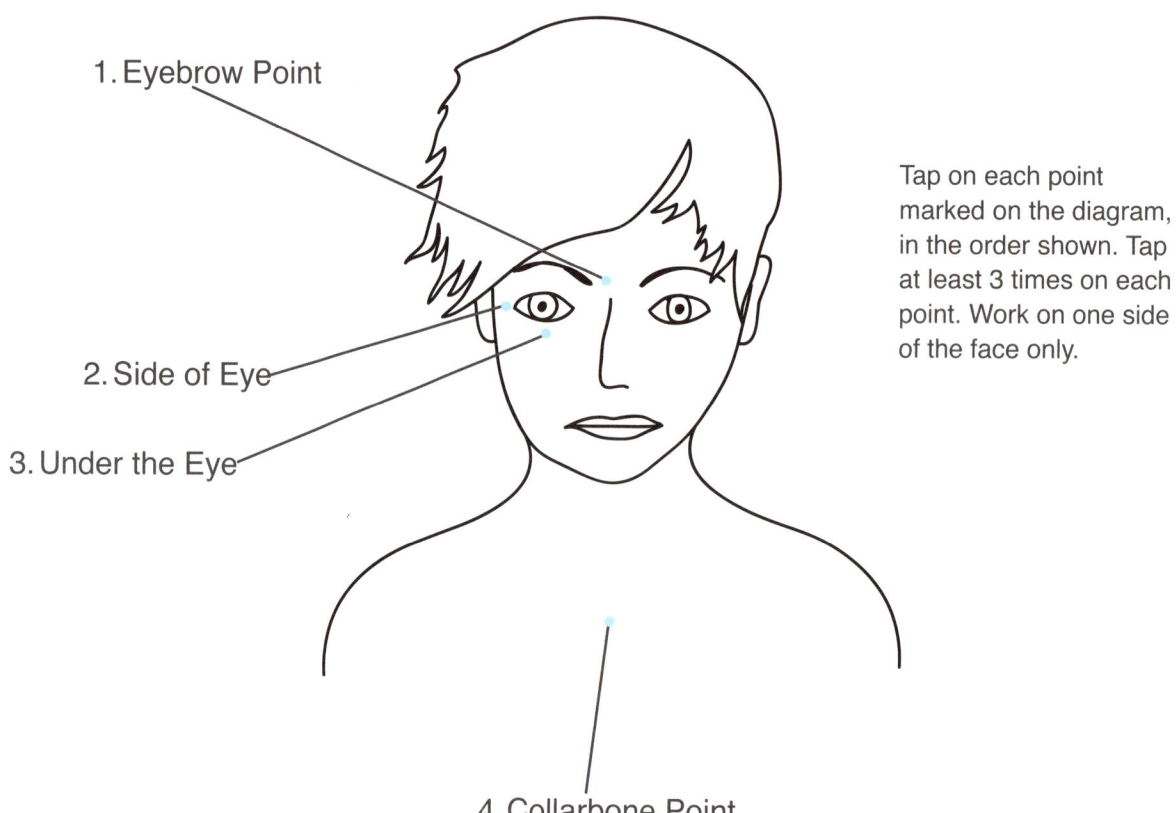

1. Eyebrow Point
2. Side of Eye
3. Under the Eye
4. Collarbone Point

Tap on each point marked on the diagram, in the order shown. Tap at least 3 times on each point. Work on one side of the face only.

5. Test the Intensity Again:

Finally, you establish an 'after' level of the emotion's intensity by assigning a number to it on a scale of 1-10. You compare this with the 'before' level to see how much progress you have made.

You may wish to continue tapping on this emotion or you may feel ready to revisit the 'emotional scale' and move along to a different emotion.

Please don't worry about finding the exact spot for tapping, the most important thing is to focus on the feeling.

Note:

Deal with one emotion at a time. Allow yourself patience as you work through these emotions. Work at your pace, rest when needed and drink plenty of water.

Wellbeing

THE CENTRE OF WELLBEING

What is NLP?:

Neuro: Our thoughts and thinking

Linguistic: Our words and language

Programming: Our behaviour and choices

NLP is simply about understanding how our minds work and how we behave, so that we can understand ourselves, and others, much better.

Being aware that we can all make changes in our thinking and behaviour, allows us to take 100% responsibility for the choices we make and to really transform our lives. In a nutshell, NLP can enable you to make positive, beneficial changes in your life.

"For things to change, *you've* got to change. Otherwise nothing much will change"

- Jim Rohn

THE CENTRE OF WELLBEING   Wellbeing

NLP Practice:

A Different Point of View

When we look at things differently our understanding, or perception, of what is happening can change. This NLP technique is great to:

• Improve your understanding of other people.

• Enable you to think more clearly.

• Provide an opportunity to consider issues objectively.

1st Perspective - See the situation through your own eyes. Run through the problem as if you are there in it. Pay attention to your own thoughts and feelings.

2nd Perspective - Imagine what it is like to be the other person. Put yourself in their shoes How is 'that you over there' coming across to you. Is he/she taking your views into account?

3rd Perspective - Imagine being a "fly on the wall" looking at yourself and the other person, pay particular attention to the body language and the sound of their voices. Then consider, as a result of taking this view, what advice you want to give 'yourself' about how you are handling the situation.

Recovery
Institute of Psychiatry, Psychology & Neuroscience Kings College London

Research into recovery

What does research tell us about recovery?

- **Recovery is an active process** – others can't make you recover
- **Individual and unique process** – your
- journey of recovery is your own to discover
- **Non-linear process** – it's normal to hit hurdles
- **Recovery as a journey** – recovery is a personal experience
- **Recovery as stages or phases** – one step at a time!
- **Recovery as a struggle** – feel good about achievements, no matter how small
- **Multidimensional process** – recovery can occur in different parts of your life
- **Recovery is a gradual process** – so be compassionate towards yourself
- **Recovery as a life-changing experience** – move forward to who you will become
- **Recovery without cure** – can involve living with, or beyond, an illness
- **Recovery is aided by supportive and healing environment** – by having helpful influences in your life
- **Recovery can occur without professional intervention** – some people find another route
- **Trial and error process** – it's okay to try and fail

What are the key recovery processes?

1. Connectedness – who or what do you connect with?
2. Hope & optimism about the future – would someone's recovery story inspire you?
3. Identity – what positive parts of your identity do you want to activate more?
4. Meaning in life – what makes your life worth living?
5. Empowerment – what can you do?

More information on recovery research is at researchintorecovery.com

Reference
LEAMY M, BIRD V, LE BOUTILLIER C, WILLIAMS J, SLADE M (2011) A conceptual framework for personal recovery in mental health: systematic review and narrative synthesis, *British Journal of Psychiatry,* 199, pp. 445-452.

Institute of Psychiatry, Psychology & Neuroscience Kings College London   **Recovery**

Research into wellbeing

What does research tell us is important for wellbeing?

Connect...
With people around you. At home, work, school or in your local community. Think of these as the cornerstones of your life and invest time in developing them. Building these connections will support and enrich you every day.

Be active...
Go for a walk or run. Cycle. Play a game. Garden. Dance. Exercising makes you feel good. Most importantly, discover a physical activity you enjoy.

Take notice...
Be curious. Catch sight of the beautiful. Remark on the unusual. Notice the changing seasons. Savour the moment. Be aware of the world around you and what you are feeling. Reflecting on your experiences will help you appreciate what matters to you.

Keep learning...
Try something new. Set a challenge you will enjoy achieving. Learning new things will make you more confident as well as being fun.

Give...
Do something nice for a friend, or a stranger. Thank someone. Smile. Volunteer your time. Join a community group. Look out, as well as in.

Reference

AKED, J, MARKS, N, CORDON, C, THOMPSON, S (2008) *Five Ways of Well-being: the Evidence.* London: New Economics Foundation.

www.researchintorecovery.com

www.kcl.ac.uk/iop

Recovery

"ImROC puts recovery at the heart of mental health services."

The Implementing Recovery through Organisational Change (ImROC) programme is a new approach to helping people with mental health problems.

ImROC helps mental health service providers change the way they work with service users and families, making them genuine partners in care. The objective is to go further than just involvement, creating a culture of working together in every aspect of the organisation's work.

ImROC supports organisations in reshaping their services to give more people the chance to recover and to fulfil their potential. With professionals on tap, as opposed to on top, and hope, control and opportunity as the core principles of mental health services, we can achieve lasting change in people's lives and life chances.

In February 2011, the Department of Health commissioned the Centre for Mental Health and the NHS Confederation's Mental Health Network to pilot the national programme with 29 NHS funded mental health service providers. It used a framework of self assessment set against 10 key challenges by which organisations might become more recovery-orientated.

The project team, consisting of leading experts in recovery and organisational change including Geoff Shepherd, Rachel Perkins, Julie Repper, Jed Boardman and Glenn Roberts, delivered over 100 on-site consultancy visits and ran 24 one-day workshops with member sites.

The second phase of ImROC was launched on 14 February 2013 with Care and Support Minister Norman Lamb MP, and is open to all NHS funded mental health service providers and local partners.

The continuing work of ImROC has received endorsement from the Department of Health and is supported by the Centre for Mental Health and the Mental Health Network.

ImROC

Recovery

At the launch event in Westminster, Norman Lamb MP encouragingly set out his support for recovery:

"Recovery and recognising that people with even the most severe mental health problems can recover is a crucial part of modern mental health services.

Through ImROC, mental health service providers are recognising that people with direct experience of mental ill health can offer just as valuable expertise as clinicians. Combined, they can gently revolutionise mental health care in this country, and ensure people with mental health problems can live the lives they want to, with strong relationships, a sense of purpose and independence."

Based on an annual membership scheme, member sites will focus on raising the standards of recovery orientated services through a series of information sharing workshops, at an annual conference, on-line through a virtual e-recovery platform and through a range of supporting consultancy packages.

Local partnerships made up of people with lived experience of using mental health services, friends, families, carers, mental health service providers and third sector organisations will carry out this organisational development work at a local level.

Centre for Mental Health
Realising a better future

020 7799 6666
imroc@nhsconfed.org
www.ImROC.org

Recovery

Royal College of Psychiatrists

Recovery is a personal process of learning how to live a satisfying and productive life with or without enduring symptoms or vulnerabilities.

Even with the limitations caused by illness, it is about gaining hope, meaning, purpose, choice and control over patterns of living valued by the person themselves. It is not necessarily about going back to how you were before you experienced a mental illness but about managing your symptoms better with, or without, medication. But it is more than this. People describe it as finding a different kind of meaning and purpose as they improve and move beyond the effects of illness.

Drivers of the recovery process:

- Finding hope and optimism
- Believing in yourself, developing meaning and purpose
- Taking control of your illness and life
- Taking opportunities to develop a meaningful and satisfying life

While some experience similar things, no two people have exactly the same way of reacting to them. Therefore, your recovery may be similar to, or very different from, that of someone else with mental health problems. Remember, it's your recovery and it's important to do what you feel is best for you and at your own pace.

Some people find that treatment controls remove their symptoms completely. For others, they remain – or fluctuate. For some, treatment does not help at all. Despite this, recovery is still possible. This means returning to a productive life even if you continue having troublesome experiences. Rather than being simply stabilised in the community, the aim of recovery is for you to be a part of it in a way that suits you. There is 'no one size fits all' approach to recovery. It will be different for each person.

Reference
LE BOUTILLIER C, LEAMY M, BIRD VJ, DAVIDSON L, WILLIAMS J, SLADE M (2011) WHAT DOES RECOVERY MEAN IN PRACTICE? A QUALITATIVE ANALYSIS OF INTERNATIONAL RECOVERY-ORIENTED PRACTICE GUIDANCE, PSYCHIATRIC SERVICES, 62, 1470-1476.

Royal College of Psychiatrists   Recovery

How can people be supported in their recovery? Key elements:

Developing good working relationships – we need to support individuals to fulfil their potential and to shape their own future. A therapeutic relationship is essential in supporting recovery where partnership working and hope is promoted.

Supporting personally defined recovery – there is a need to focus on this and view recovery as being at the heart of practice and not as an additional task. Individuals are supported to define their own needs, goals and plans for the future to shape their care content.

Organisation support – people do not work in isolation and need support from their employing organisation. Recovery principles should run throughout it. Recovery-supporting services show a commitment to promoting recovery-oriented practice and provide a culture that focuses on, and adapts to, the needs of people rather than those of services.

Promoting citizenship – aims to support people who live with mental illness to live as equal citizens. Citizenship is central to supporting recovery where a right to a meaningful life for people is advocated.

Co-production, informed choice, peer support, a strengths focus, and social inclusion are all parts of recovery.

020 7235 2351
www.rcpsych.ac.uk

Recovery

Manage your stress levels

Being in a stressed state of mind a lot of the time can make us overreact or feel negative.

Managing stress can be a gradual process so begin by taking a look at your lifestyle. If you have a lot of stress in your life, find ways to reduce it, such as asking your partner to help with chores in the house, taking a relaxing yoga class, or talking to your boss about changing your working hours.

Another step can be to introduce some form of regular exercise and to set aside some time for yourself, for example, to take a bath or listen to music. Taking control of your time in this way can effectively reduce stress.

It can be easy to rush through life without stopping to notice much but when you pay more attention to the present moment; you can improve your mental wellbeing.

This awareness is often called: 'mindfulness' and you can take steps to develop it in your own life by becoming more aware of the present moment. In simple terms, this means noticing the detail of every moment: the sights, smells, sounds and tastes that you experience, as well as the thoughts and feelings that occur from one moment to the next.

Mindfulness can help us enjoy the world more and understand ourselves better.

NHS choices

Recovery

Relaxed breathing for stress

If you have feelings of anxiety alongside stress, then breathing exercises and relaxation can help to relieve the symptoms. It can help you calm down and take a step back from a stressful situation.

Although the cause of the anxiety won't necessarily disappear, you will probably feel more able to deal with it once you've released the tension in your body and cleared your thoughts. Don't worry if you find it difficult to relax at first. It's a skill that needs to be learned and it will come with practice.

Good relaxation always starts with focusing on your breathing. The way to do it is to breathe in and out slowly and in a regular rhythm as this will help you to calm down:

• Fill up the whole of your lungs with air, without forcing. Imagine you're filling up a bottle, so that your lungs fill from the bottom.

• Breathe in through your nose and out through your mouth.

• Breathe in slowly and regularly counting from one to five (don't worry if you can't reach five at first).

• Then let the breath escape slowly, counting from one to five.

• Keep doing this until you feel calmer. Breathe without pausing or holding your breath.

Practise this relaxed breathing for three to five minutes, two to three times a day (as required).

www.nhs.uk.

Meet The Panels

Chair of the Art/Photography Assessors Gary Hodges:

"Being a judge on the 'rethinkyourmind' competition has been very rewarding although sometimes frustrating! I say that because we judges were not just choosing the best artworks, but the best 'uplifting' artworks. There were so many entries to the competition that were brilliant, but sadly didn't quite fit into the required 'uplifting' criteria.

Also there were some amazing artworks that if it had been for an actual three dimensional exhibition in a gallery, we would have picked them straight away. However, we were choosing the art that would look best in the two dimensional 'Yellow Book'.

I can't wait for the next 'rethinkyourmind' competition to see what beauties emerge from imaginative hearts, hands and minds."

Chair of the Poetry Assessors Lydia Towsey:

 "This year the standard of writing submitted to rethinkyourmind made shortlisting and then picking the final winners extraordinarily difficult. Though all of us agreed on the final cut, many of us also had our own other individual favourites that we weren't able to put through – I'll continue to remember some of these pieces and be glad to have read them. The work was by turns innovative and heartfelt, insightful and above all uplifting. Poetry in the UK is alive and well."

Gary Hodges

Gary Hodges is the chair of the rethinkyourmind art and photography panel and is the UK's best selling and most collectable pencil artist. He has sold nearly 110,000 signed and numbered printsfrom 128 limited editions. Only 12 of these editions are still available from his website.The huge demand for Gary's prints has led to a lucrative secondary market. Greenpeace published his first print in 1987 (edition of 850) which sold for £8.50 each. In recent years "Green Turtle" has changed hands for up to an incredible £3,500.00

The many accolades given during his 35 year career include the "Oscars" of the published art world, the "Best selling Artist of the Year" awarded by the Fine Art Trade Guild.

His many thousands of admirers include: Virginia McKenna, Martina Navratilova, Pam St Clement and Rula Lenska. Gary's massive popularity has enabled him to follow his heart and support charities dear to him. Through his art well over half a million pounds has been given back to protect the wildlife he feels so passionate about.

www.garyhodges-wildlife-art.com

rethinkyourmind.co.uk   Art Assessor

Keith Cooper

Keith Cooper is a Leicester based professional, commercial and architectural photographer who combines his creative abilities with the very latest technical developments in photography.

His recently exhibited 14 metre photographic print of Leicester City Centre at dusk, pushed the limits of photographic and printing technologies, whilst retaining the sense of space and light that embody and characterise his more conventional landscape photographs.

His technical expertise is reflected in the test and development work he does with major manufacturers in the photographic and print markets. Keith's passion for passing on his photographic skills is clearly shown in the articles and reviews he writes for his website.

It is Keith's photographic images and recognised technical expertise that have helped make the Northlight Images web site one of the top 40 photography web sites in the world.

We would like to thank Keith for submitting pieces from his extensive gallery to help create the wellbeing section.

www.architecture-photos.co.uk

Steven McLoughlin

Steven McLoughlin was born in 1970 and is a self-taught artist. Showing a serious interest in art from the age of 16, Steve initially drew pencil portraits.

A flair for fine architectural drawings led Breedon Books to hand Steve his first commission at the age of 19, illustrating a series of street scenes of Old Derby.

That eye for detail was also drawing Steve to wildlife subjects and also landscapes.

Steven has been painting professionally for over 10 years and during this time has become experienced in using many different mediums.

He spends a lot of time on the coast, walking the North Norfolk and Cornish coastlines as well as the Derbyshire countryside where he lives.

'I am aiming to provide an illusion of space and tranquillity by painting open skies and landscapes. I find pastels and acrylics give me the subtlety and depth I need to achieve.

www.steven-mcloughlin.co.uk

Jenny Escritt

Jenny Escritt is a Photographer and Printmaker who lives and works in Birmingham.

After gaining a degree in Fine Art in 1979, where she specialised in printmaking, Jenny developed an interest in experimental photography, mostly using cameras (including pinhole experiments and Polaroid manipulation), and also exploring non-camera based techniques such as painting with darkroom chemicals and hand coloured photograms.

She has a particular interest in experimenting with the viewer's perspective, using blur, reflection, focus and camera angle to spur enquiry and evoke emotional response.

More recently Jenny has concentrated on monoprint and etching experiments, using similar ideas and reference points to those used in her photography, and exploring different kinds of mark making and stencil effects.

www.jennyescritt.com

Art Assessor

Lucia Masundire

Lucia Masundire has been working in arts development for 7 years working at Leicestershire County Council, having studied Arts Management at De Montfort University. She is a trustee and Senior Fellow for Arts Development: UK, as well as Leicester Print Workshop the centre for fine art printmaking in the Midlands.

Her current project Click; Connect; Curate; Create is exploring how digital can be used to increase engagement with museum collections.

www.connect-curate.com

Poetry Assessor

Lydia Towsey

Lydia Towsey is the chair of the rethinkyourmind poetry assesor panel. She is a poet and performer with a Masters in Creative Writing.

Her previous commissions include: Poet in the City's Spoken Word All Stars Tour; Beyond Words — U.K. tour of four South African poets (Apples and Snakes) and Sole2Soul (University of Leicester). Lydia has been shortlisted for the Bridport Poetry Prize (2012) and has performed at London's 100 Club. She has been published by The London Magazine, Hearing Voices and Magma Magazine, amongst others. Her work is included in *10 Poems about Knitting* (Candlestick Press) and *Raving Beauties – Hallelujah for 50ft Women anthology* (Bloodaxe Books). Her full length collection, *The Venus Papers* is published by Burning Eye Books (2015).

In 2015 she continues UK touring *'Three the Hard Way'* - alongside Jean Binta Breeze and Shruti Chauhan (www.3thehardwaypoets.wordpress.com).

Lydia is Arts in Health Coordinator at Leicestershire Partnership NHS Trust; Chair/Compere of WORD! - the longest running poetry night in the Midlands (www.wordpoetry.eu) and Chair of Brightsparks (www.brightsparks.wordpress.com).

www.secretagentartist.wordpress.com

Jean 'Binta' Breeze

Jean 'Binta' Breeze is an internationally renowned Jamaican poet and playwright, well known for her mastery of the 'dub' artform. Her words carry powerful political and personal messages, and audiences relate to and are inspired by her work.

She is the author of many poetry collections most recently *Third World Girl* (Bloodaxe) which combines writing from previous collections and new poems.

Her former awards include a NESTA and a Writing Fellowship at the University of Leicester.

Now based in Jamaica, Ms Breeze tours England in spring and autumn with producers renaissance one, and as part of an event marking International Women's Day, has appeared on BBC World Service's The Forum.

In 2012 she was a recipient of an MBE for Services to Literature. Watch performances of Jean and enquire about her at the website below:

www.renaissanceone.co.uk/jean-binta-breeze

Adam Horovitz

Born in 1971, Adam Horovitz has been active as a poet since the 1990s, treading a fine line between page and performance poetry.

He released his first pamphlet, *Next Year in Jerusalem*, in 2004 and a second, *The Great Unlearning*, in 2009. He was the poet in residence for Glastonbury Festival's official website in 2009 and was voted onto the Hospital Club 100 in 2010 as an emerging talent. His debut collection, *Turning*, was released by Headland in 2011.

He was awarded a Hawthornden Fellowship in 2012. In 2014, he released *A Thousand Laurie Lees*, a verse-fuelled memoir from The History Press, and *Only the Flame Remains* (Yew Tree Press) and was one of five British poets selected by Ledbury Poetry Festival in 2015 to be part of the pan-European Versopolis project.

www.adamhorovitz.co.uk

Moniza Alvi

Moniza Alvi was born in Pakistan and grew up in Hertfordshire.

After working for many years as a secondary school teacher in London, she is now a freelance writer and tutor, and lives in Wymondham, Norfolk with her husband and daughter.

Her first two collections were published by Oxford University Press: *The Country at My Shoulder* (1993), shortlisted for the T.S. Eliot and Whitbread poetry prizes and selected for the New Generation poetry promotion, and *A Bowl of Warm Air* (1996).

Her later poetry titles have all been published by Bloodaxe Books and include *Split World:* Poems 1990-2005 (2008) and *Europa* (2008) and *At the Time of Partition* (2013). Both these last two books were Poetry Book Society Choices shortlisted for T.S. Eliot Prize.

In 2002-04 she was a trainee at the Westminster Pastoral Foundation studying counselling and group analysis.

www.moniza.co.uk

Helen Ivory

Helen Ivory is a poet and assemblage artist. Her fourth Bloodaxe Books collection is the semi-autobiographical *Waiting for Bluebeard* (May 2013).

She has co-edited with George Szirtes *In Their Own Words: Contemporary Poets on their Poetry Salt* 2012.

She edits the webzine Ink Sweat and Tears and is tutor and Course Director for the new UEA/Writers Centre Norwich online creative writing programme.

A collaborative Tarot pack with the painter Tom de Freston is due from Gatehouse Press in 2015 and she is currently working on a book of collage/cut-up poems for Knives Forks and Spoons Press.

www.helenivory.co.uk

Russell Thompson

For the last decade, Russell Thompson has worked for Apples and Snakes, England's leading organisation devoted specifically to the advancement of live poetry.

As such, he has devised tours, theatre shows and artist-development initiatives.

Russell is a seasoned performing artist himself, appearing both as Rachel Pantechnicon and as one half of the pop-and-poetry duo Project Adorno.

In these guises, he has featured on BBC Radios 1, 3 and 4, and has appeared on the bill of events as diverse as WOMAD and the StAnza Poetry Festival.

www.applesandsnakes.org

www.projectadorno.net

Poetry and Art
Selected Entries

The following pieces of art and poetry were created with the focus of
"I feel better when I am…"

- Rethinkyourmind opened for entries on 14-11-14 and closed on 15-3-15.
- 280 entries were assessed and 50 pieces were selected for The Yellow Book.
- 14 of these 50 were further chosen to feature in our music singles and album:

  - 4 single covers from artwork entries
  - 2 album covers from artwork entries
  - 4 lyrics from poetry entries
  - 4 spoken word B sides from poetry entries

Music Artists

How would it feel if your poem was used to create lyrics or a spoken word 'B' side of a project single?
Especially if it was also creatively supporting mental health...?
Music adds another dimension to the project!

Here Are The 4 Music Artists For 2015

As lead singer with The Bluetones Mark enjoyed a 15 year recording career that produced 6 studio albums, 3 of which achieving Top 10 sales in the UK, including the #1 album 'Expecting to Fly', 13 Top 40 singles, and a Brit nomination in 1996. Mark has recorded 2 solo albums and music for various side projects, including the Title and Chapter music for the 6 audio book versions of David Walliams' children's stories. Mark was also a judge on the Album of the Year panel for the Ivor Novello Awards.

www.markmorrissmusic.co.uk

Lucy Ward is an award winning acoustic artist from Derby. After winning the Horizon Award for best newcomer at the 2012 BBC Radio 2 Folk Awards, Lucy's career has gone from strength to strength. In 2013 it was announced that she had been nominated for the acclaimed "Folk Singer of the Year" at the 2014 BBC Radio 2 Folk Awards, making Lucy one of the youngest people ever to be nominated for this most prestigious award. Her album 'Single Flame' became MOJO #2 Best Folk Album 2013.

www.lucywardsings.com

Music Artists

How would it feel if your artwork was used as a cover for a project single or album?

Especially if it was also creatively supporting mental health...?

Bringing selected entries to life in 4D!

Here Are The 4 Music Artists For 2015

Refuge are an acoustic band with Pete, the project creator of 'rethinkyourmind' on vocals, Sam on bass and Phil on guitar and backing vocals. Their latest album 'Moving Inwards' features the single 'Reflections' which was played on BBC Introducing. This latest album was mentored by Mark Morriss, lead singer of 'The Bluetones' & Gaz Birtles of 'The Beautiful South' as part of a project that is making live music an everyday feature on mental health hospital wards.

www.musicfromrefuge.co.uk

OLIVIA ROSE DEANE

Olivia Rose Deane is a Leicester based singer songwriter who has long written music and songs for herself and has recently discovered that other people like listening to them too. As well as a few gigs and performing at Edinburgh Fringe; Olivia has also released her debut single "Sally" and getting ready to record the next.

www.oliviarosedeane.com

Selected Album Front Cover

'Silhouette' by Rebecca Hayes   (Pontypool)

Selected Album Back Cover

Andy Gardiner (Tiverton)

I Feel Better When

I feel better when I am watching for spring
Daffodils open and make my heart sing.
I feel better when writing beautiful words
Inspired by nature filled with returning birds.
I feel better when I am painting a glorious sky
The sunset has colours to make the spirit fly high.

I feel better when I am grateful for simple things
Each day has a moment touched by angelic wings.
I feel better if I take a walk in a wood
There is something about green that makes me feel good.
I feel better when I think of the natural world
Where flora and fauna are free and unfurled.

Maria B Potter (Lancashire)

'When I'm Smiling' by Nik Bragg (Stroud)

Selected Music Single Lyrics

It is a Place ………

It is a place

I know I belong

It is a place

I feel safe

It is a place

That accepts me as I am

It is a place

That loves me unconditionally

It is a place

Where I am left alone with thoughts

It is a place

That keeps me safe

It is a place

Where I am known

It is a place

That allows me to take responsibility for myself

It is a place

Where I see me as me

It is a place

That allows me to leave my worries at the door

It is a place

I know as home

Sohaib Mirza (Halifax)

Lucy Ward

rethinkyourmind.co.uk Selected Music Single Cover

'Grounded' by Liat Wicks (Rochester)

Selected Music Single Lyrics

A Dream In The Storm

I feel a flight of fancy
And want to carry you away
Out of a world of despair
Into a beautiful day
Where you smile and you laugh as you should
do
And the sun and the sky light your face
So that fields of misfortune forget you
And there's no misery in this place
Jagged edges in life which have hurt you
Where you feel yourself start to cry
I've been there before and I've felt this
So let me dry that tear in your eye
I'm nought but the dreamer I'll grant you
But dreams are the things you deserve
If you wake with a smile in the morning
Well, then the purpose is served.

Des Mannay (Newport)

rethinkyourmind.co.uk Selected Music Single Cover

'Quiet' by Emily Quinn (Peterborough)

My Tangled Mind Set Free

Now I'll tell you a true story
About a man, who, once lost his mind
He was dealt a wrong hand
A fate too unkind

We met up in a coffee house,
In Old Leicester Square
It become a physical attraction
A friendship we begun to share

He'd say; Pretty girl be kind to me
Sunrays and moonbeams entwine with me
Let the stars shine down on me
You've set my tangled mind, free

The summer rays, shone down on us
As we strolled hand in hand,
through London town
Big Ben chimed loudly
He fooled around, acting the clown

He said, with you, I hear birds sing
I feel the sunbeams on my skin
This world is a now a brighter place
Girl you've such a pretty face

He said girl, come dance with me
And the truth as it be
I fell in love with him
He fell in love with me

He whispered, let's build a little house
It'll be our Buckingham Palace
I'll be your Christopher Robin
You'll be my breathtaking Alice

We stay strong through our misty days
Life's recovered in many ways
It was meant to be, some how
Our journeys, forever now
So life is about true love

For oneself and for others
We all need love
And we became lovers

Years on were still together
He loves me, just the same
He now calls himself Tarzan
And me Lady Jane

So now the true story ends
Giving hope and inspiration to you
You could be me
And he could be you
He said;

Pretty girl, be kind to me
Sunrays and moonbeams entwine with me
Thanks for the stars that shine down on me
My tangled mind set free

Denise Claxton (Grays)

OLIVIA ROSE DEANE

Selected Music Single Cover

'Loved' by Mair Eleri Davies (Pontardawe)

Swimming Out To The Rock

I awoke feeling ready to go – give it the large, swim out to de rock.

It was sunny morning with a nice breeze, gave me the feeling of ooh u know, it can be my day.

Anyhow, mum was washing clothes as usual. Kwik brekky then gt a trans to the beach. Yeah man, arrival was good and the beach was quiet. Early morning stylee.

Anyway i was up for it, in other words. Got changed and put one ft in afta the other in the tepid blue coloured water, naturally.

Swimming out to da rock stroke by stroke giving my body a necessary work out.

Floating out yonda distance, hearing the hooters of boats big and small and de early fishermen awaiting a catch.

Boats coming into the harbour with holiday makers looking onwards.

My experience to de rock was like havin a lyme n njoyn ma skin, peace.

Ian Liburd (Leicester)

Snow White

Drudging for dwarves
is much overrated, thinks Snow White.
Tedious little ones who expect me
to do it all. And as for waiting for a prince
to bail me out (and wash his socks),
I really don't think so.
I don't like this story.
Forget the Prince!
Delete the Dwarves!
I'm going to dance in fountains
drink champagne and eat sweet peaches
climb high mountains
laze on beaches
drive fast cars.
whiz down slopes of stars.

Susan Castillo Street (Mayfield)

A Salad

Today I make
a salad–
The red flesh of tomato
gives way to the blade;

The moisture of
cucumber;

The crunch of
yellow pepper–
a spurt of flavour;

The lettuce–
sculpted,
cut,
bounces back.

I cry at its life,
its beauty,
its availability to me.

To me!
Today I see God.

Katherine T Owen (Swindon)

Library

I find myself huddled
In the reference section of the library
Where silence reigns supreme
Where books rule the landscape
In neatly orderly rows
Organisation collection of information
Residing on shelves
On subjects beyond my understanding
On subjects beyond my vocabulary
I arrive here early
Position myself and my belongings on the table
Select a book from the shelf
Open it
Begin to read
Until I understand the meaning
Until I can feel the pain, the passion
Until I can visualise the landscape of the written word
I stop only to sneak in a sandwich
Rules forbid this
But I have mastered the craft
Then I start reading again
Until 5pm today
When the library closes.
I shall be here again tomorrow

Waseem Mirza (Halifax)

Etymology

"I feel better when I am…"
It begs a thousand endings.
 The romantic: "…with my beloved"
 The practical: "…fed and warm"
 The humorous: "…probably not a newt"
 The holy: "…struck far reeling by zip-
 crunch-sting of frost on my feet and
 night on my teeth and the stars and
 the stars and the stars and the-"

 The start can also be a complete
 sentence.

 "I feel better when I AM", you see,
 when I am me and my self is
 brewed strong hot and in the world,
 when the ghost world (doubting)
 leaves no worse footsteps then,
 oh, THEN…
  I am.
   Do you see?
    The me I am
     and how much better that feels?

There's an end tucked in there too.
(after the fretting and restringing)
(the mistaken misshapen missteppings)
(the whithers/ whethers/ whatevers all
 noise and gasping no I no see)
 Therein lies a neat universe, coiled.
 There, the sleek contented arrival at
 journey's root:
  "I FEEL, better, when I am".
  I feel, alive (breathe)
  I feel, strong (eat)
  I feel, deep (drink)
   For one breakout heartbeat, under
   sky, over earth, I…
   I feel… more than Before.
   I feel… more than Ever.
   (and love)
   (Love)
   Love
    LOVE

Anna Nic Giolla Mhuire

(Galway, Republic of Ireland)

'Misty the Westie' by Katy Young (Flintshire)

Butter

*I feel better when I eat butter
I go nuts for pats on garden peas
even though it makes me fatter
I love it on crackers, under cheese*

Lauren Foster (Loughborough)

'Tea fixes everything' by Emily Quinn (Peterborough)

Paper Plane

I sit under the shade of velvet leaves,
pale tint of orange pours over the field.
Lately I have been finding fresh shoots
amongst the withering wildflowers of the past.

I have written a farewell letter to my Pain
and folded it like a blanket. Even if I am uncertain
like the crumpled laughter of the river
I must go straight ahead…

The velvet leaves rustle. The patches of light
dancing on my face somehow make me smile.
My paper plane drifts further and further –
sharp nose towards the burning edges of the clouds.

Romalyn Ante
(Wolverhampton)

'Autumn Birch' by Toni-Ann Green (Leicester)

Bubbles

The first 9 stretch out from the wand
Each one, plum sized, quivering gently
Propelled on a gentle mid-June breeze
moving randomly across suburban scenery

I take my time with the next blow
A pair of oranges, rainbow smeared
each one holding a reflected me
One glides away, doomed from the start
the other, disappears against a cotton
sleeve

Blowing as if flickering a candle flame
I produce 28 gooseberries that saunter
off like bees
Some mark the bark, some glisten
the leaves
and the last few assail and
escape over the trees

I try out my next trick and conjure 2 apples
fused as a conjoined twin
This double-bubble hovers and shimmers
waiting for me, but it's a booby trapped globe,
exploding causing shrieks of glee

I contemplate producing a grapefruit
When a tug on my arm, small outstretched hand
other resting on a hip, disarms me begrudgingly
I hand over the bottle with a sheepish grin
and the soapy coated, orange plastic,
dipping stick

Lee Prosser (Llangyndeyrn)

Katharine Elizabeth Jennings (Forest Row)

Tabla

Rhythm of the music is pure and divine.
It remains in you and me. Helps to make some peace.
The tabla gets battered but gives you pleasure –
Dha dhin dhin dha dha dhin dha
dha tin tin ta tak dhin dhin dha.
That's the language but for me it's my treasure.
Musical instruments are gifts from God
through which we connect to ourselves, each other.

Repetition of hand movements
create the fascinating sound of the Tabla,
put mind at ease and pause in thoughts,
help calm me down and know myself.
Powerful beats of Tabla piercing through,
connecting ear with heart and soul.
The battle inside stops for a while
giving me the pleasure of winning.
I rise from the feeling of being small
and I roar like a lion,
accept all the challenges.

Jitendra Bhatt
(Leicester)

'F Block' by Gary Molloy (London)

It Does Us Good

The sky is big in Wiltshire.
The buildings fall away
the eye adjusting to
a wider landscape.

It does us good:
we expand our vision.

We let nature breathe in us –
touching maybe joy,
maybe sadness, but
touching.

It does us good:
we feel our feelings.

The Wiltshire Downs are
big enough to hold us.

It does us good:
let us be held.

Katherine T Owen (Swindon)

'Immersed in Nature' by Liat Wicks (Rochester)

Hands Poem

*Your marshmallow hands,
squishy talcum powder hands.
Your closed crab claw hands,
your tiny ten times smaller
pink hands saucered in my palm.
Smooth young unscratched,
unblemished skin, fingers curled,
hanging on hands.*

*Your dinky pinkies, your gooey
jelly baby hands, cotton wool
balls of hands, fluffy rabbit paws,
soft cream, ice cream hands,
clasping ,clutching, cosseted, closed
in mine, warm as dumplings hands.
Teeny weeny huggy bear hands,
precious to us both hands..*

*John Saunders
(Tullamore, Republic of Ireland)*

'Summer Rain' by Dovilė Anoškaitė (Peterborough)

This Cinderelly Nonsense

Home is where the heart is, they say,
  They who are not me or you or anyone we know
    Yet I think they got it right, just a little right this time.

  Home is where the hearth is, you say, joking,
    While the flames lick warm orange around us
      And I think there must, there surely must be magic in these slippers.

      Home is where the heart's hearth smoulders.
        That space where you curl up, a sleepy comma on my chest,
          While I think, "ach there's no place, there is no place so sweet"

Anna Nic Giolla Mhuire
(Galway, Republic of Ireland)

'New York City' by Ashley-Marie Wall (Loughborough)

Across the Leam from Mill Gardens

The clock drips from the parish church.
As I cross the bridge
to Jephson Gardens
it is early February
and the pigeons remain unfed by council
decree.
 "Mind your head"
 the entrance to the underpass reads
 the only piece of graffiti left in this oh so
 heavenly place.
  Mothers walk their babies
  this as every morning in Royal
  Leamington Spa.
   Operatives tend the grounds
   to ill- afford the prices in this town so
   high.
    "A Lady with dirty petticoats"
    alongside Edinburgh
    once described, a fairytale town
    with Cinderella absent,
    a beauty with a mole or two.
     But, did Victoria with all her
     majesty foresee
      that behind all the façades and the
      remnants of imperial glory
       lingers young people robbing the
       well-heeled for the next hit?

Leamington, my home, that saved me a
spiral downwards......
Now I rise ever mindful of the pitfalls,
ever mindful of knowing my position
in the order of things.

John RT Yates

(Leamington Spa)

'Better when walking near trees and water' by Jenny Meehan (Chessington)

Rainbow

Red berries
  Smile
    Beside storm-curdled mud-drifts;
     Birds pecking land and worms back from fenced waterfields.

      Russet brown and orange – requiem saw shavings
       From the old tree brought down across the pavement.
        Only a livid stump remains
         In its allocated earthbreak;
          Its sentinel centuries
           Blown
            Dust.

But
  Marigold flowers
   Humbly swarm to warm the bottom of a gate post,
    And the yellowing green of new catkins
     Hangs a promise above greying ghosts;
      Shade-slumbering old man's beard
       Tangles winter's last legacy into a hedge,
        Bequeathing tufts, but only here and there,
         To the blinking blue sky.

    Down the road,
     Indigo grasses have been newly planted in proud garden pots,
      Whilst crocuses sprinkle the park;
      Violet,
       Like the memory
        Of lavender
         In brush-dry broken branches
         Piled ready for burning,
          Now colour has come back to us.

            Deborah Hyde
            (London)

'The time to blossom is now' by Bibi (Birmingham)

Night Swings

It's grey clouds
piled together,
like a thick, threatening pillow.
And black sky,
burping thunder.

It's a swarm of youth;
dark hoods and hard tongues
buzzing playfully
like locusts,
Under a willow tree.

It's sodden grass
under feet
and porridge mud
with thick toffee skin.
It's the moon above me,
yellow, thick, and throbbing,
like sky's blister.

It's rusty chains
and green poles
that creak.
And feet becoming wings
which launch me.

It's a haunting sky.
Feral hair
whipping rain in lashes
on my face
and falling into thunder
feet first.

It's leaving earth.
Becoming black clouds
and mist.
And For one moment,
It's feeling big.

It's letting go,
It's jumping.
And landing in a pile of legs
and grazed skin
and smiles.
It's conquering again

Sian Breeze (Chalford)

'Sunset at sea' by Toni-Ann Green (Leicester)

Wordly Pleasures

Out of the blue they tumble, spilling
across the page, shouting, thrilling
to their own songs and sounds, rattling
the gates of convention, battling
to be heard – scattering everywhere
in shapeless masses, in triplets and pairs,
on envelopes and newspaper margins,
on menus, post-its and paper napkins.
A rag-bag of words, a verbal maze,
a couplet or two, a peach of a phrase.

From the chaos of this wordly storm
the semblance of a verse is born,
shy at first, with unsteady feet,
with thoughts and metre incomplete,
with unfit rhymes and erratic style,
with story lines unreconciled.
And it is my pleasure to soothe and nurse
the growing pains of this youthful verse;
lost in the tangles of these troubled lines
I find myself,
free from the tangles of a troubled mind.

Trish Kerrison (Belper)

'Walking Forward' by Alex Thompson (London)

Morning Run

The stars are visible even at dawn.
I breathe the scents of morning dew,
stretch my arms wide open.

My red trainers are worn-out
but a new smile gleams on my face.
Forget the race of life, I run at my own pace.

I kick the pain away
like an empty can.
The breeze strokes my cheeks

My lungs expand...
I listen to the chirping of sparrows,
forget the static noise in my earphones.

I let my heartbeat slow down
under the graceful gliding of petals
from a cherry blossom tree.

Soon I feel the sunlight on my back,
your tap on my shoulder.

Romalyn Ante
(Wolverhampton)

'Big Tree' by Andy Wild (Kirkby Lonsdale)

Do You Remember

Do you remember that summer?
 Together in Corsica
  We drove the winding roads
   Through the coral sunbeat mountains
    To the coast of Cargèse.
     I'll never forget the beach
      Where we laughed together for hours
       On that peaceful afternoon.
        We were the only ones
         Lying there
          You, me, mam and pap
           And oh how we laughed at her – a mummy
            Wrapped like that, in her cream pashmina
             Hiding from grains that danced with the wind
              And at him
               For, well… just being him
                In those shorts and with that hat
                 Do you remember?
                  Running on the warm sand with me
                   To where the little boats lay tired and thirsty

We sat on their edge
 Drawing stars in the sand with our toes
  And we left them there
   As a thank you note for the night sky
    For always being there to wish upon
     So when I need to, I go back there
      Back to Corsica
       With you
        Between the mountains and the sea
         Dancing on those little boats
          Where all that mattered was just
           to be

Lisa de Jong
(Dublin, Republic of Ireland)

'Gratitude' by Elisabeth Svanholmer (Mytholmroyd, Hebden Bridge)

The Wall

On the other side,
they think I'm better
when
I'm medicated,
and I'm on a
hospital
ward,
but every brick
of that wall
has helped put me here.
I feel better when the newspapers
report boring headlines.
And Twitter is trending
about real stories,
not myth or
mystery.

I feel better with my lover when
we sail along the river.
And I tremble at the
thought I have
succeeded along
the way with
her help.
And I feel fine, when
I am walking through the streets,
and the street is not walking
through me, because
everybody knows
I am an actor not simply
a spectator of life, and
there is no wall
to pin me in.

I'm always on the other
side of that wall,
no matter
what they
think and I'm
fine because I have more than
the wings of a prayer.
And no barrier is
high enough
for me.

David Holloway
(Bedford)

'Sunrise in London' by Carole Baker (Carshalton)

Bruce Lee

*Bruce Lee knocks on my front door.
He was all in white.
The angel said, Carlton
I've come to bring you some precision
in your training. Carlton, Carlton
I've been watching you in your living room,
you have my powers.
So he came in and sat down
and we practiced together.
We worked on precision
and prayers together
We worked on coordination
control and meditation.
I said, Bruce Lee
there are lots of things
I'd love to ask
but a warrior never knows
when it's done.*

Carlton Anthony Brown (Leicester)

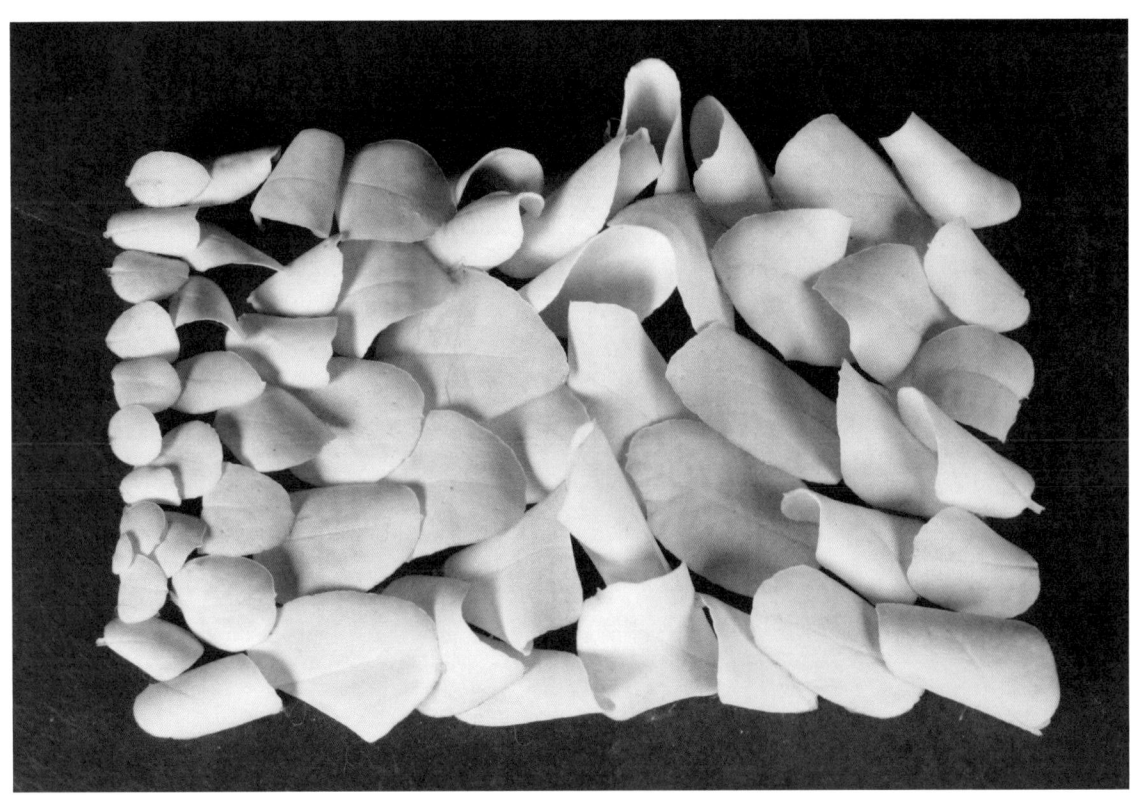

'Eucalyptus' by Jo Keogh (Leicester)

Change

*Five months later,
leaving the ward,
staring up at the sun,
and wondering,
'will my new life
be like my old'.*

*A year later…
No more suiciding.
A new flat.
Old friends.
New friends.
Volunteering.*

*I look forward
and I look back.
I think and I over-think.
All I can truly say
is that I'm not better,
but I am recovering.*

David Rollins (Leicester)

'Sunshine in the rain' by Annie Watkinson (Yateley)

The Small Things in Life

A laugh with a friend or a long journey's end
The warmth of a bath on a cold winter's night
An extra hour's sleep or good food going cheap
A difficult test and you get it all right.
The sand in your toes and your comfiest clothes
The point you can breathe at the end of a cold
A day of good hair and a soft comfy chair
The moment your naughty dog does as it's told.
A gripping new book or the days others cook
A new episode of your favourite show
An afternoon nap and some big bubble wrap
The childish excitement at seeing fresh snow.
A comical joke where you laugh till you choke
An unforeseen text from an old long-lost friend
A hug from your spouse and a wholly clean house
The absolute joy of a stressful day's end.
A good cup of tea or a splash in the sea
When two snack bars fall in the vending machine
A pillow's cool side or the times scissors glide
A drive through a town where all lights are on green.
A good reminisce or a soft gentle kiss
The moment warm water hits freezing cold hands
Your favourite song and to sleep all night long
A small local concert with epic new bands.
The view of the stars or the smell of new cars
A dip in a pool on a hot summer's day
Removing tight shoes and good things on the news
A big homemade cake from a little cafe.
The sight of sunsets or a cuddle with pets
A Saturday where you don't have to get dressed
A freshly made bed or the smell of baked bread
The small things in life are so often the best!

Katy Young
(Flintshire)

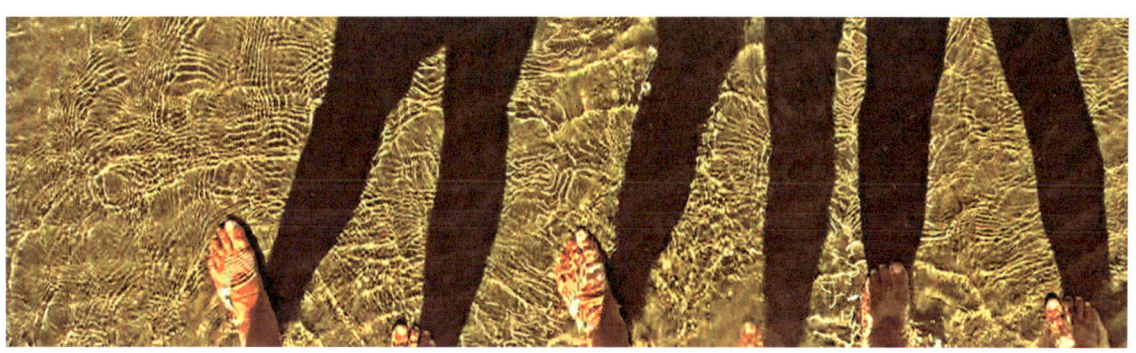

'Rhythms' by Willow Merryweather (Nottingham)

The following pages are dedicated to signposting national supporters.

National Supporters

rethinkyourmind.co.uk

Advance offers an unrivalled breadth of services for people with disabilities or mental health conditions, including housing, specialist support, brokerage and employment.

From our beginnings in 1974 we have enabled people to live the lives they choose at home, at work or in the community.

Advance works with more than 4,000 people across 42 local authority areas.

We are proud to support the Rethink Your Mind project as part of our commitment to innovative practices and initiatives in the field of recovery and mental health.

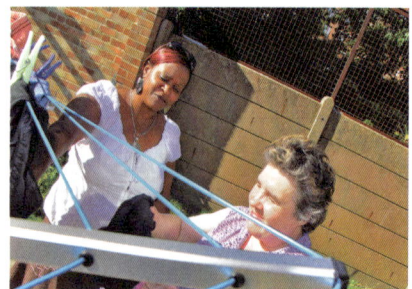

 0333 012 4307

 info@advanceuk.org

 www.advanceuk.org

rethinkyourmind.co.uk

National Supporters

Bipolar UK is the national charity dedicated to supporting individuals with the much misunderstood condition of bipolar, their families and carers.

Established in 1983 to combat the lack of dedicated services, service user participation is core to everything we do.

We provide support services for individuals affected by bipolar including a national network over 120 self help groups, a moderated 24/7 online peer support forum, mentoring and a specialist youth support for people aged 18 to 25.

We provide information and guidance, work in partnership with research organisations and seek to combat the stigma and discrimination.

We supported more than 70,000 people last year and demand for our services continues to rise.

020 7931 6480

info@bipolaruk.org.uk

www.bipolaruk.org.uk

National Supporters

rethinkyourmind.co.uk

BAMT is the professional body for music therapists and a source of information, support and involvement for the general public. BAMT works locally and nationally to promote and raise the profile of music therapy in the UK.

Music therapy is an established clinical discipline which is widely used to help people of all ages whose lives have been affected by injury, illness or disability.

The unique properties of music therapy mean it has the potential to play a vital role in sustaining the health and wellbeing of our society into the future.

Priority areas of public health, care and social wellbeing, such as maximising opportunities for vulnerable children, improving adult mental wellbeing and caring for the growing number of people affected by dementia.

To find out more about music therapy and how you can be involved, please contact us.

 020 7837 6100

 info@bamt.org

 www.bamt.org

rethinkyourmind.co.uk

National Supporters

Centre for Mental Health

Centre for Mental Health is a charity which aims to help to create a society in which people with mental health problems enjoy equal chances in life to those without.

We believe that people with mental health problems should not experience unfair barriers to a fulfilling life.

We carry out research, policy work and analysis to improve practice and influence policy in mental health as well as public services.

We aim to find practical and effective ways of overcoming those barriers so that people with mental health problems can make their own lives better with good quality support from the services they need to achieve their aspirations.

 020 7827 8300

 contact@centreformentalhealth.org.uk

 www.centreformentalhealth.org.uk

National Supporters

rethinkyourmind.co.uk

You may well be aware of the benefits of a healthy and active lifestyle, but fitting in healthier eating and more physical activity can often feel like an uphill struggle. Yet with Change4Life it needn't!

For the last three years, we've been committed to providing regular hints and tips on how to make simple, straightforward life-changing swaps, which all add up to a positive, health enhancing transformation.

We're already helping over 500,000 families across the UK, and with your support we could help even more.

We have an extensive range of useful information and materials that you can use to communicate the benefits of healthy eating and activities for all ages and levels of ability.

✉ C4LPartnerships@dh.gsi.gov.uk

🖥 www.nhs.uk/change4life

rethinkyourmind.co.uk

National Supporters

ChildLine on 0800 1111 or www.childline.org.uk is the UK's free, confidential helpline dedicated to children and young people.

Whenever children need us, ChildLine will be there for them - 24 hours a day, 7 days a week, 365 days per year.

At ChildLine bases around the UK, trained volunteers are on hand to provide advice and support 24 hours a day.

Children can get in touch either by phone on 0800 1111, or online at www.childline.org.uk – whichever makes them feel most comfortable.

Direct support online is provided through live 1-2-1 chats and email.

0800 1111

www.childline.org.uk

National Supporters

rethinkyourmind.co.uk

Community Innovations Enterprise (CIE) provides tailor made programmes that provide innovative solutions to a range of community and social inclusion issues e.g. increasing service access to a more diverse range of communities; understanding demographic and locality based changes in community needs and aspirations; developing frameworks for action and innovation in equality and human rights.

CIE aims to go beyond traditional customer insight programmes or community consultation services by placing the communities or client groups in question at the heart of the chosen development.

We also support organisations to reach diverse communities while at the same time increasing their capacity and capability to achieve meaningful engagement and promote social inclusion.

 jon@ciellp.com

www.ciellp.com

rethinkyourmind.co.uk

National Supporters

Depression Alliance is the leading national charity that works with people who experience depression and anxiety.

We are recognised and respected in the health, welfare and charity sectors for our knowledge and expertise in a wide range of effective methods of non-medical support for depression.

We run a successful network of self-help groups across England, publish a quarterly magazine, coordinate a pen friends scheme and host an online chat forum DATalk.

We have piloted and now run wellbeing projects in London built around Time banking.

Informed by the experiences of people with depression, we also raise awareness of the realities of the illness amongst the general public with a variety of influential campaigns throughout the year.

0845 123 23 20

information@depressionalliance.org

www.depressionalliance.org

National Supporters

rethinkyourmind.co.uk

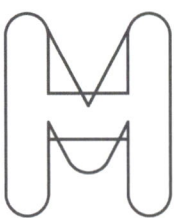

We are working for an end to mental ill health and the inequalities that face people experiencing mental distress, living with learning disabilities or reduced mental capacity.

We develop and run research and delivery programmes across the UK that have, for more than six decades, given us the evidence and expertise to know what works and how to intervene earlier.

We influence policymakers and advocate for changes in services, using firm evidence and the voices of people with direct experience of the issues.

We work across all age ranges and all aspects of mental health. We are the charity for everyone's mental wellbeing.

 020 7803 1100

 info@mhf.org.uk

 www.mentalhealth.org.uk

rethinkyourmind.co.uk

National Supporters

MHPF is the leading representative body for voluntary sector providers of mental health services, with over 60 members drawn from national, regional and locally based organisations operating across England.

A total of 5 million people were supported across our membership last year and we continue to work towards making recovery for those living with mental ill health a reasonable and attainable goal.

MHPF is a platform for collaboration and co-operation in areas of joint concern and interest. It also acts as a combined single voice for the mental health voluntary sector, facilitating communication from and to government bodies.

We are united by our desire to improve the quality of care for people with mental health needs and the outcomes of services provided.

0207 253 7556

www.mhpf.org.uk

National Supporters

rethinkyourmind.co.uk

The NHS Confederation's Mental Health Network (MHN) is the voice for mental health and learning disability service providers to the NHS in England. It was established as part of the NHS Confederation in 2007.

The MHN represents providers from across the statutory, private and third sectors and works with Government, NHS bodies, parliamentarians, opinion formers and the media to promote the views and interests of its members and to influence policy on their behalf.

Joining the MHN provides members with access to regular policy briefings, reports and news bulletins, full access to the MHN website where members can download information and documents on current hot topics in mental health and book onto 'member-only' events.

 020 7799 8702

 mentalhealthnetwork@nhsconfed.org

 www.nhsconfed.org/mhn

rethinkyourmind.co.uk

National Supporters

Get Connected is the UK's free, confidential and multi-issue helpline for under 25s who need help and don't know where to turn.

Our service is available 365 days a year over the phone, via webchat, email and text, plus we have a searchable online directory of support services and a free help app.

When a young person gets in touch, our trained Helpline Volunteers offer emotional support and can let them know about further specialist help from a database of more than 9,000 trusted organisations. We're free, we're friendly, we don't judge and we won't tell.

 0808 808 4994

 help@getconnected.org.uk

 www.getconnected.org.uk

National Supporters

rethinkyourmind.co.uk

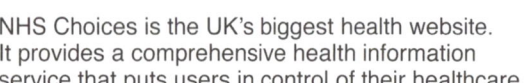

NHS Choices is the UK's biggest health website. It provides a comprehensive health information service that puts users in control of their healthcare.

The website helps users make choices about their health, from decisions about their lifestyle, such as smoking, drinking and exercise, to finding and using NHS services in England.

NHS Choices includes around 20,000 regularly updated articles. There are also hundreds of thousands of entries in more than 50 directories that can be used to find and choose health services in England.

 www.nhs.uk

 www.nhs.uk/aboutNHSChoices/Pages/ContactUs.aspx

rethinkyourmind.co.uk

National Supporters

NSUN network for mental health is the only England-wide charity led by, and for, people with experience of psychological distress.

We link service-users to each other and to carers, health professionals, commissioners and policy makers in order to ensure that people have the greatest possible influence over the services they use and their own lives.

Nationally NSUN sits on the Department of Health Ministerial Advisory Group on the Mental Health Strategy and many other influential bodies.

It's free to join us and members get a weekly emailed bulletin with all the latest mental health news, jobs and opportunities; a regular printed newsletter and invites to free events and training. Join today because together we are stronger.

 0207 820 8982

 info@nsun.org.uk

 www.nsun.org.uk

National Supporters

rethinkyourmind.co.uk

Rethink Mental Illness is a charity that believes a better life is possible for millions of people affected by mental illness.

In 1972, one man spoke about his family's experiences of mental illness in a letter to the Times and in the process brought together hundreds to talk about their experiences of mental illness and support each other. Today we directly support almost 60,000 people every year across England to get through crises and rebuild their lives.

We give information and advice to 500,000 more and we change policy for millions.

We are a membership organisation, governed by people who have lived through mental illness.

 0121 522 7007 - Members, Donors And General Enquiries

 0300 5000 927 - Advice and Information Service

 info@rethink.org

 www.rethink.org

National Supporters

A totally confidential, anonymous conversation with a stranger can often feel easier than talking to someone you know.

Sometimes you can't talk to family or friends about what's weighing on your mind. That's where we come in.

 08457 90 90 90

 jo@samaritans.org

 www.samaritans.org

National Supporters

rethinkyourmind.co.uk

SISO - Safe Inside Safe Outside - is a service user led Social Enterprise which helps people to feel safe within themselves and their wider community. We have developed a Toolkit for Wellbeing, full of leading edge, easy to use techniques to help make the Recovery Journey a reality.

SISO seeks to reduce stigma and inequalities associated with mental and emotional health challenges, looks at the Whole Person and promotes Hope and Optimism.

SISO offers the very best in Positive solutions for a wide range of challenges. We specialise in Emotional Freedom Technique and utilise West African drumming

Contact us for more information about our training programmes, workshops and resources.

07447 961220

info@s-i-s-o.org.uk

www.s-i-s-o.org.uk

rethinkyourmind.co.uk

National Supporters

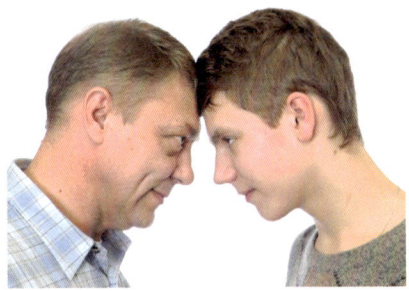

Completely free and always impartial, the Money Advice Service was set up by government to help everyone manage their money. Its advice is available online, on the phone, or in person, through a UK-wide network of expert Money Advisers.

Its website at moneyadviceservice.org.uk has over 500 easy-to-use guides, action plans, comparison tables, and calculators to make managing your money easier.

If you'd rather have a chat, its Money Advisers are standing by to answer any question you might have about any of life's money matters on 0300 500 5000.

The organisation is completely independent, so you can trust what it says - it doesn't sell or recommend any products or companies, but offers free advice to help you make informed choice that are right for you.

 0300 500 5000

 enquiries@moneyadviceservice.org.uk

 www.moneyadviceservice.org.uk

National Supporters

rethinkyourmind.co.uk

Time to Change is England's biggest programme to end the stigma and discrimination faced by people with mental health problems.

The programme is run by the charities Mind and Rethink Mental Illness, and funded by the Department of Health and Comic Relief.

We aim to work with all sectors and communities to encourage more open conversation about mental health and ensure that people with mental health problems can be equal and active citizens.

Time to Change combines a national campaign with community activity.

We fund grassroots anti-stigma projects through our grants scheme, and support people with experience of mental health problems to become active social leaders.

We also work with the media, a wide range of organisations, BME communities and children and young people.

 020 8215 2356

 info@time-to-change.org.uk

 www.time-to-change.org.uk

rethinkyourmind.co.uk

National Supporters

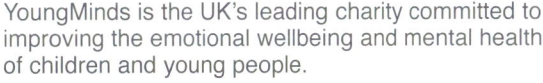

The voice for young people's **mental health and wellbeing**

YoungMinds is the UK's leading charity committed to improving the emotional wellbeing and mental health of children and young people.

Driven by their experiences we campaign, research and influence policy and practice.

We also provide expert knowledge to professionals, parents and young people through our Parents' Helpline 0808 802 5544, online resources, training and development, outreach work and publications.

The YoungMinds Parents' Helpline offers free confidential online and telephone support, including information and advice, to any adult worried about the emotional problems, behaviour or mental health of a child or young person up to the age of 25.

 020 7089 5050

 ymenquiries@youngminds.org.uk

 www.youngminds.org.uk

National Supporters

rethinkyourmind.co.uk

student minds

Student Minds is the UK's student mental health charity. We believe that peer interventions can change the state of student mental health. We deliver research-driven training and support to equip students to bring about positive change on their campuses through campaigning and facilitating peer support programmes.

Our vision is for all universities and health services to recognise positive mental health as a priority for student success. We want students to take action to foster an environment where everyone has the confidence to talk and listen to each other, the skills to support one another and the knowledge to look after their own mental health.

 01865 264168

 hello@studentminds.org.uk

 www.studentminds.org.uk

rethinkyourmind.co.uk

National Supporters

READING WELL

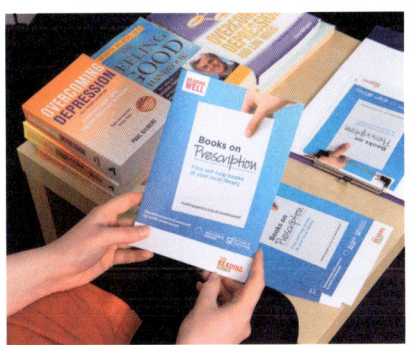

Reading Well Books on Prescription is the new national scheme for England delivered by national charity The Reading Agency in partnership with the Society of Chief Librarians, local library services and health partners. The programme provides self-help reading for adults based on cognitive behavioural therapy for a range of common mental health conditions, including anxiety, depression, phobias and some eating disorders. The programme also now supports people with dementia and their carers, with a reading list launched in January 2015.

Reading Well Books on Prescription is supported by the Department of Health (IAPT), Royal College of General Practitioners, Royal College of Psychiatrists, Royal College of Nursing, British Association for Behavioural and Cognitive Psychotherapies, British Association for Counselling and Psychotherapy, National Association for Primary Care, The British Psychological Society and Mind.

The Reading Well programme also offers Reading Well Mood-boosting Books - a national promotion of uplifting novels, non-fiction and poetry, selected by readers and reading groups around the country.

 0207 324 2544

 readingwell@readingagency.org.uk

 www.readingagency.org.uk/readingwell

National Supporters

rethinkyourmind.co.uk

healthwatch

Healthwatch England is the national consumer champion in health and social care. We have significant statutory powers to ensure the voice of people is strengthened and heard by those who commission, deliver and regulate health and social care services.

Health and care are critical lifelines to many millions of people every year. It can be a bewildering environment and often we use services when we are vulnerable or fearful.

Healthwatch is the only part of the health and social care system whose sole purpose is to voice the concerns of those who use services. We are here to champion children, young people and adults in England so they are as powerful as the services they use. We work for everyone, not just those that shout the loudest.

 03000 683000

 enquiries@healthwatch.co.uk

 www.healthwatch.co.uk

rethinkyourmind.co.uk

National Supporters

Support and friendship for families

Home-Start is a leading family support charity that helps parents to build better lives for their children. Our volunteers provide support and friendship to more than 29,000 families every year.

Our highly trained volunteers offer support for parents with young children to cope with pressures caused by isolation, mental ill health, multiple births, bereavement, disability, poor housing or financial stress.

Volunteers visit a family's home for a couple of hours every week and the support they offer is tailor-made to the needs of the parents and children.

Families are supported until the youngest child turns five or starts school, or until the parents feel they can stand on their own two feet.

There are 288 local Home-Starts in communities across the UK.

 0800 068 63 68

 info@home-start.org.uk

 www.home-start.org.uk

National Supporters

SPOTLIGHT ON SCHIZOPHRENIA

• **Georgina Wakefield** •

Georgina Wakefield has been on both sides of the fence having been a Mental Health Service User since the age of 18 and a carer to her youngest son Christian who suffers from Schizophrenia for the past 23 years.

An Accomplished public speaker she has also written several books and taken part in 10 films in order to obtain training materials which she uses to deliver "From The Carers Perspective" at various NHS Trusts Universities and The Institute Of Psychiatry where her work has earned her Honorary Lecturer status.

"I have become a Campaigner in order to raise the profile of Mental Illness and gain respect for those unlucky enough to become part of something that is no more than a tragic life event".

spotlightonschizophrenia@yahoo.co.uk

www.georginawakefield.co.uk

rethinkyourmind.co.uk

National Supporters

MovinginWards.co.uk

Moving InWards is making live music an everyday feature on mental health hospital wards, particularly focussing on intensive care units and forensic settings. Originally funded by the Arts Council England, the project is now a part of Develop-Insite CIC. Project lead, Pete Hirst, uses his earlier experiences of being an in-patient to help provide hope and support to those on the wards.

The work is delivered by the acoustic band 'Refuge' and they provide:

- Music Performances
- Singing & Ukulele Workshops
- Staff Training Packages to ensure sustainability

Beginning in August 2014, this project was successfully piloted with the support of Leicestershire Partnership NHS Trust:

"There were so many therapeutic benefits to these sessions." **Belinda Jordon - Herschel Prins Centre**

"It was really refreshing to see such a large majority of the patients engaging in the music session and thoroughly enjoying it and having fun."

Jo Lock - Ward Matron - Watermead Ward

 contact@movinginwards.co.uk

 www.movinginwards.co.uk

 01279 868500

 email@markdavid.co.uk

 www.markdavid.co.uk

A family business with over 30 years' experience in designing and delivering beautiful German and handmade fitted kitchens.

Our values are rooted in bringing the kitchen vision of our clients into reality and to ensure the whole experience is as seamless as possible.

We understand that the initial disruption of installing a new kitchen can be stressful and we are keen to signpost clients to all that the 'rethinkyourmind' project has to offer and supply them with their very own Yellow Book.

 0116 2327400

 hello@cwa.co.uk

 www.cwa.co.uk

CWA is a creative marketing agency with over 40 year's experience. We advise and develop marketing communication materials for our clients in the field of design, digital and live event communications. What sets us apart is the way we work.

To get in touch with the people at CWA use the contact details above.

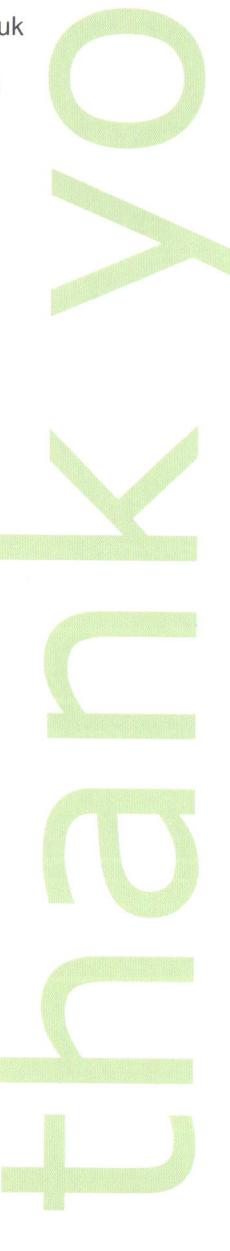

Thanks to Peterborough Regional College for all the time and support with the project this year. The student and staff participation in the project was wonderful especially as some now feature among our winners.

In addition to stocking hardcopies of The Yellow Book, a personalised, online yellow book has also been created for the college to enable it to reach more of the student population and showcase their work. There is a positive focus on wellbeing within the college which aligns with the 'rethinkyourmind' project.

We are grateful to the college for piloting this concept so that other colleges/schools/universities may do the same.

Leicestershire Partnership
NHS Trust

Our thanks to Leicestershire Partnership NHS Trust for their continued support of 'rethinkyourmind' and The Yellow Book.

They have been on-board since the Project's inception and have made The Yellow Book widely available throughout their services.

Graphic Design

Our thanks to Primal Mistry for devoting his time and skills to The Yellow Book 2015, his support has been fantastic and we have been very grateful to be working alongside such an accomplished and up and coming graphic designer.

www.behance.net/PrimalMistry

PRIMAL MISTRY
GRAPHIC DESIGNER

We owe such gratitude to the previous designers who willingly gave their time to help and support the work. To Tanya Goodwin for her wonderful eye for detail and her tireless enthusiasm around all aspects of the project. To Kat Price for her support developing the promotional material and Lucy Crewe for her fantastic animation skills. We thank you all.

www.creativecatfx.tumblr.com

We would also like to say a huge thank you to Lisa Newell whose fantastic brand and graphic design skills have made rethinkyourmind into an accessible and user friendly resource for everyone.

Web Design

Lisa Ward of Fresh Web Creations, deserves so much more than our words of gratitude for embracing the rethinkyourmind vision and significantly developing the website into a brand new operating system in readiness for this year's competition.

www.freshwebcreations.com

We would like to thank Joe Davine for his support in enabling the transfer of the website in 2014.

Deep thanks are sent to Shelly Maddox, of shellymadesigns, for originally creating and developing the rethinkyourmind website, her generosity and selfless support throughout the process was wonderful.

Music Recording

We are delighted to be working with Adam Ellis at Deadline Studios in Leicester for all the recording, mixing and mastering of the 'rethinkyourmind' music and spoken word poems. His expertise in this field is second to none and we are privileged to be working alongside him.

www.deadlinestudios.co.uk

Photography - our thanks to:

Project Photography:
Scott of Choucino Photography, Leicester, for cataloguing the journey of rethinkyourmind 2015 featured on our rethinkyourmind website.

www.scottchoucino.com

Book Photography:
Keith Cooper 'Art Assessor' – Page 'Welcome', 8, 10, 11, 13, 18, 24, 27, 34 and 35
Elaine Dawes – Page 12, 14, 15, 16, 21, 28, 40, 42 and 43
Rich Wakefield – Page 17, 22 and 23
Kat Price – Page 37, 39 and 41
Photograph of Pete Hirst and Claire Ramsbotham by Scott Choucino
Photograph of Moniza Alvi by Steve Lyne
Photograph of Lydia Towsey by Ambrose Musiyiwa
Photograph of Gratitude Jar by Julie Cluff of www.stampingjulie.com

Wellbeing

Wellbeing section written by Claire Ramsbotham in collaboration with:

Linda Swanton – Special thanks for the emotional scale
Debbie Walmsley – Special thanks for the NLP practice
Nikki Robinson – Special thanks for the 'Stretch' piece
Carol May – Special thanks for the gratitude practice
Tana Macpherson-Smith, Nicola White, Joy Gravestock, Sherry Palmer, Julian Harrison, Cherry Stuart, Anne Hirst, Natalie Cheary, Gilli Fawcett.

Our thanks to all those that provided such wonderful 'feedback for our friends'

P.R.

Natalie Cheary thanks for your passion towards the project, and for writing and disseminating such authentic articles.

Gonoral Support

Samantha Maddin- sincere thanks for all your assistance with the online shop and your general enthusiasm to be of help.
Marilyn Johnson- many thanks for your admin support throughout rethinkyourmind 2015.

And Finally…

Our deepest gratitude to Fran Singer for her dedication and support in gaining the recognition for this project by the top institutions in the field of mental health.

And huge thanks to all the team at SISO (Safe Inside Safe Outside), Leicester – a personal thank you from Pete for all your support and guidance over the years and for allowing him to change the direction of his life, particularly through this project.

And here on the final page of The Yellow Book, some may say that we have reached the end of our journey together…

However, as a Mindfulness Coach, I would remind you that the journey of growing and learning never ends!

It is our sincere hope that you will dip in and out of this book and enjoy its contents, throughout your journey of life.

My journey took a dramatic U-turn about 5 years ago and I was fortunate to be connected with the practice of mindfulness. This practice became my teacher and then my passion and my belief in its potential to support others led me to qualify as a Coach.

Since those early days, I have now opened The Centre of Wellbeing to ensure that wellbeing options are better understood and more accessible whilst providing people with a safe and quiet space to practise.

When I met Pete in 2014, we were united in our belief that wellbeing practices support empowerment and maintain wellness. We have now set up Develop-Insite CIC together to facilitate projects that creatively support positive mental health and we continue to be open to growing and learning along the way.

Thank you for being with us & may your journey be all that you choose. In love and kindness,

Claire
Develop-Insite CIC: Managing Director